TABLE OF CONTENTS

INTRODUCTION

We are excited to develop this amazing weight management e-book for you. I have never been a person to struggle with my weight. Before having my first child in 1997 I was barely 115 pounds. Graduating from high school I was barely 100 lbs. So, you see, weight was never an issue.

Some people tend to blame the weight gain on having children. Well, I think I am going to piggyback on that one, but that will not last forever. I have made up my mind to get out of the Moan Zone and start being accountable for whatever happens to my body. The only person that can change you is you.

Food is no longer a necessity in my eyes. The necessity is to give your body the nutrients that it needs. Yes, yes, food is very good, but your body does not need or want all the fatty stuff that is incorporated inside food.

If you are going to start being wise and eat based on nutrition, then you need to get your family members to eat for nutrients as well. Do not allow anyone to stop you from obtaining your goal of getting in shape. If I can do it, you can do it. What I am about to show you is not a diet, in fact,
it is a new way of healthy eating. You will feel yourself having more energy to do the things you have wanted to do your whole lifetime.

In this weight management e-book, you will learn how to eat, exercise, and not feel like you are pressured. You will need some Will Power, but you can do it.

Get read, Get Set, Let's make a change

Click to Purchase

Acknowledgments

First, I give all honor and glory to God. God allowed me to be birthed on this day for this purpose and I am grateful. I want to thank the following people in my life:

My mom, Mary Williams, who is now deceased, for allowing herself to be used as God's vessel to get me here. You showed me how to be a true independent woman. I am grateful.

My father, Frank Williams, for allowing God to use him as a vessel as well. You taught me how to be a strong woman and an entrepreneur at heart. It is in my blood. You taught me how family should stick together no matter what - I am grateful.

My husband Keith for being a super husband. You have taken care of me and loved me from the very beginning. Every idea that I have ever had you have supported me. Each time I called myself fat you told me how beautiful and sexy I was to you. I love you for that and I am grateful.

My children, Joshua, and Wendi for being the best children a mother could ever ask for. You are always there to care and help me. You are God's gift to me, and I love you guys forever and a day. I am grateful.

My friend, Cindy Rodriguez-Williams for being my friend. You also allowed God to use you to come into my life at IHP. We never know our purpose in life, but I know God had a purpose when we crossed paths. You and Marcus came over to our home one evening for dinner and you were a bit harsh, but you told me "you have to be 100% committed if you want to lose weight." This book is my commitment and I am grateful.

A fellow student in my School of Ministry class told of a story about her friend that wanted to lose weight, but that she wanted to eat what she wanted. This story

about resonated deep in my soul. She told her friend,
"what you are telling me is the same as you saying you
want to become a changed person and go to church,
but you want to keep sinning; you can't do that - - either
you jump in or get out of the boat."

This lady had no idea that she was used by God to help
me make up my mind and start eating the way I should
have been eating long ago. Thank you, my sister, - I am
grateful.

Prayer/Scriptures

Prayer has gotten me though numerous trials in my lifetime. Trials come to make us strong. I have faith that the following Scriptures will help you as well:

John 15:5 "I am the vine, you are the branches; he who abides in Me and I in him, he bears much fruit, for apart from Me you can do nothing."

Philippians 4:13 - I can do all things through him who strengthens me.

Matthew 6:25 *"Therefore I tell you, do not be anxious about your life, what you will eat or what you will drink, nor about your body, what you will put on. Is not life more than food, and the body more than clothing?*

1 Corinthians 6:19-20

Or do you not know that your body is a temple of the Holy Spirit within you, whom you have from God? You are not your own, for you were bought with a price. So, glorify God in your body.

3 John 1:2

Beloved, I pray that all may go well with you and that you may be in good health, as it goes well with your soul.

1 Corinthians 10:31

So, whether you eat or drink, or whatever you do, do all to the glory of God.

Proverbs 3:5
Trust in the Lord with all your heart, and do not lean on your own understanding

Self-Contract

I,_____________________, agree to duly perform everything I possibly can pursuing my weight loss goals:

Current Weight:______   Date: ________

Weight Loss Goal for this Agreement: ____

Target Weight:______   Date:

I,__________________________, hereby commit to starting today to achieve the weight loss that I know I want and need to feel good about myself. I wholeheartedly take sole responsibility for my weight and am willing to make permanent changes in my eating and exercise habits to live a healthier lifestyle.

Starting today and moving forward, I will no longer be denied the success I deserve. This is an important day in my life, the day I make the final commitment to do what needs to be done, to consistently focus on my goal and eat healthy, every hour, every day, every week moving forward. I will no longer make excuses or justify my current unhealthy eating habits and lifestyle.

I understand that my weight loss goal is going to be reached by developing new healthy habits over a period. I understand that I will not have to settle with my current weight. I have the power to change my relationship with food to one that supports my desire for a new healthy lifestyle.

Date: ___________________

Signature of Commitment

____

By signing this contract, I understand that my future is my responsibility and I am willing and capable of achieving my goal.

Habakkuk 2:2 – Then the LORD said to me, "Write my answer plainly on tablets, so that a runner can carry the correct message to others.

Any articles, posts or comments on this site should not be interpreted as medical advice. Before you begin any type of diet, make sure you consult with your physician. All images are copyright their respective owners.

Let's Get Started On Your NEW Lifestyle Journey

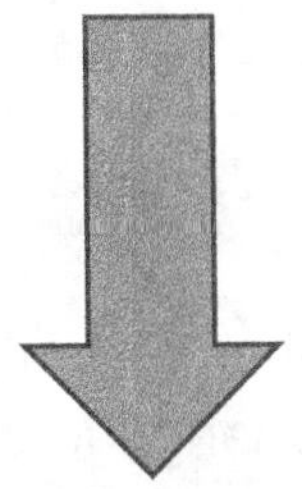

Why Should I Eat Healthy?

Why should you eat healthy? That is a good very good question. For beginners, your body requires certain nutrients that are only found in healthy nutritious foods.

Eating these foods allows your body to function properly. The essential nutrients your body needs include:

- ✓ protein
- ✓ carbohydrates
- ✓ fats
- ✓ vitamins
- ✓ minerals
- ✓ water

Eating healthy is not as difficult as you might think. There are so many fad diets and theories on the market today.

Not only are the fad diets slapping you in the face every time you turn around, but also, there are nutrition stores trying to lure you in with their suggestions. Sometimes, it can be difficult to know what to believe and where to find reliable information about healthy eating.

A Healthy Diet:

- Protects you against the effects of aging
- Increases energy levels
- Reduces risks from certain health conditions and chronic diseases, such as cancer, osteoporosis, heart disease, overweight and obesity

Nutrients: IS what a Body Needs

Chemical substances in food that have specific functions in your body, such as providing energy and helping you to grow and fight off infections are called nutrients. Like a car needing gas, timely oil changes, and planned maintenance to run properly, your body needs nutrients to continue functioning at an optimum level.

Nutrients include:

- ✓ Proteins
- ✓ Carbohydrates
- ✓ Vitamins
- ✓ Fats
- ✓ Minerals
- ✓ Water

Protein:

Is one essential nutrient in your body that makes up more than 50 percent of your total weight. Your nails, hair, skin, muscles, and organs consist of mostly protein.

A few reasons why protein is an essential nutrient.

- It helps you maintain and build strength
- It fights off infections
- It helps the body grow
- It repairs and builds healthy cells
- It supplies the body with energy.

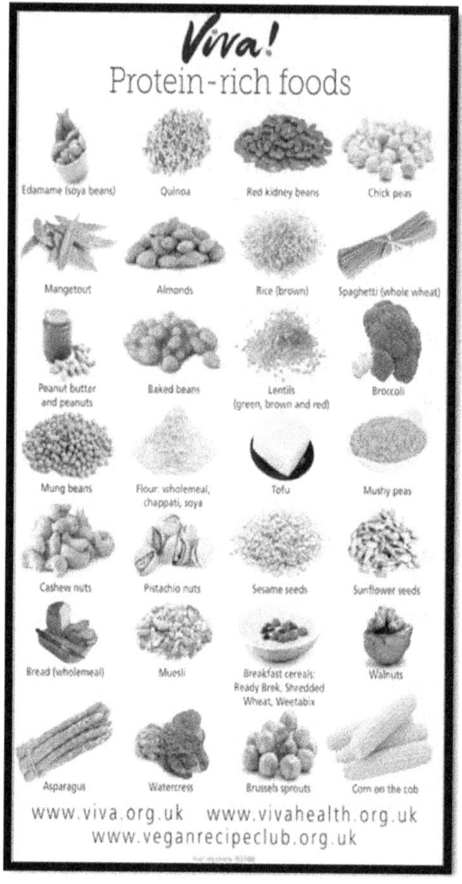

Sources of Protein

- ✓ lean red meat
- ✓ chicken
- ✓ fish
- ✓ nuts
- ✓ legumes

Dairy products like cheese and milk also are good sources of protein.

Eggs get a bad rap, but it is one of the best sources of protein. The protein in eggs has the essential mix of amino acids needed by the human body to build tissue.

Eggs also contain 13 essential vitamins and minerals.

Note: Whether an egg is brown, or white is not that important. The difference between the two are: Brown eggs come from hens with red feathers, and white eggs come from hens with white feathers. There is no difference in the nutrition the egg offers.

Most Americans usually consume much more protein than the body requires.

Carbohydrates

Bread: eat it or NAH? Pasta: empty calories* or essential nutrient? Cookies: unhealthy indulgence or necessary comfort food?

What do all the above foods have in common? For one thing, they are ALL sources of carbohydrates.

Carbohydrates (aka CARBS) are another essential
nutrient. Carbs are the primary source of energy for
humans, although protein and even fat also are
sources of energy.

Carbohydrates fall into two categories: simple and
complex. Carbs are naturally produced by plants
and animals.

High Glycemic Foods = 70+ (STOP - Try to Avoid)
Moderate Glycemic Foods = 55-69 (Use with Caution)
Low Glycemic Foods = 0-54 (GO - Ideal to Consume)

Is it Simple or Complex?

Simple carbohydrates are sugars. They taste sweet and provide quick energy. These sugars are found naturally in fruits, honey, and milk, but also can be added to foods during processing. Examples of processed foods with sugar include candy, desserts, and soda.

Complex carbohydrates, such as starches and fiber, provide your body with long-lasting energy. Most of the calories you eat should derive from complex carbohydrates.

Starchy foods: include pasta, rice, bread, and potatoes. Fruits, vegetables, and grain products such as whole-grain breads, cereals, pasta, and rice are also good sources of fiber.

Fiber

The importance of Fiber in your diet:

Fiber aids your body in moving food through your digestive system, preventing constipation. Fiber also assists in controlling your weight: It fills you up, so you are less likely to overeat. It improves the efficiency of the large intestine, keeping the muscles of the large intestine strong.

Another good aspect of fiber is that it lowers your blood cholesterol, which reduces your risk of developing heart disease.

Finally, fiber controls diabetes, and plays an important role in the prevention of colon cancer.

Recommended Daily Fiber intact amount:

The most recent version of the Dietary Guide for Americans recommends consuming 14 grams per every 1,000 calories consumed.

Is it possible to eat too much fiber?

Most popular American foods are not high in dietary fiber. When choosing a cereal, check the food labels for a cereal with five or more grams of fiber per serving. Also, when buying breads, try to purchase whole-grain breads, such as:

- ✓ Whole-wheat bread
- ✓ Rye bread
- ✓ Oatmeal bread
- ✓ Pumpernickel bread
- ✓ Cracked-wheat bread

Each of these contains more fiber than the heavily processed white breads. It is important to read labels carefully. Make sure you only buy breads that are labeled *whole* wheat. If the label simply states "wheat," it is probably high in sugar as well.

Fat:

Fat is also a nutrient. Fat provides long-lasting energy. It also helps the body store vitamins. Fast helps protect vital organs like your heart, kidneys, and liver. It also helps keeps your body warm.

It is very important not to confuse ingesting fat in
one's food with the condition of being fat; that is, being
overweight or obese. Humans *need* fat in their diets.

It is both the quantity and kind of fat that can
complicate matters.

Consuming too much fat can lead to obesity,
high cholesterol, and heart disease.

Fat stores more than twice the calories than an equal
quantity of protein or carbs. One gram of fat provides
nine calories; one gram of protein or carbs provides
four calories. This means that fat, which is still a
source of energy, adds twice the number of calories to
whatever you are eating.

What foods have fat in them? Short answer - Most.

Sometimes you can see the fat, such as in butter,
margarine, oils, lard, and creamy salad dressings. It is
the stuff that rises to the top and looks oily.

Other times you cannot see the fat, such as in sweets
and baked goods. Fats often add flavor, aroma, and
texture to food, especially in meats. Hence, the reason
why we like it so much.

VITAMINS

Vitamins are a group of nutrients found in living plants
and animals. Although, vitamins do not provide
energy like other nutrients. Instead, vitamins work to
release energy from fat, carbohydrates, and proteins
that are present in the foods you eat.

Vitamins also assist in forming bone and tissue and help your cells to function properly. Here is a scary, but real thought.

"Without vitamins, you eventually would die."

Your body makes small amounts of the vitamins you require. Therefore, most of the vitamins you need must be consumed through your food intake.

Get Your Essential Vitamins we recommend:

- ✓ Bone Health, Lower Blood Pressure - D3
- ✓ Immunity and Metabolism - Zinc
- ✓ Vitafusion Gummy - Women
- ✓ Vitafusion Gummy - Men
- ✓ Boost Immunity/Tame Inflammation - Elderberry

<u>Breakfast</u>
1 Scrambled/Fried Egg White 2 pcs Turkey Bacon
1 pc Raisin Bread (Ezekiel Bread/Gluten Free)
½ tsp Almond Butter (Spread on Raisin Bread)

<u>Snack</u>
1 Boiled Egg – NO YOLK
1 Turkey Weiner Handful Almonds/Nuts

<u>Lunch</u> Meat
Small Salad* (NO DRESSING only Fresh Squeezed Lemon as dressing)
Veggie of your Choice

<u>Snack</u>
1-Turkey Weiner w/mustard 1 String Cheese
1-Yogurt

<u>Dinner</u>
Grilled Chicken Breast
½ or whole Sweet Potato (½ tsp Agave Sweetener) Beans

Drink at least 10 glasses of Water a day

1 Corinthians 10:31 So, whether you eat or drink, or whatever you do, do all to the glory of God.

Week 1-6 - (Day 2)

<u>Breakfast</u>
2-Boiled Egg Whites
1-pc Raisin Bread (Ezekiel Bread/Gluten Free)
½ tsp Almond Butter (Spread on Raisin Bread)
1 Organic Banana

<u>Snack</u>
1-Pcs small Turkey Patty w/mustard Handful Almonds/Nuts

<u>Lunch</u>
Fish (Salmon, Tilapia, Catfish) – BAKED, GRILLED, or PAN SEARED ONLY
Spinach
Veggie of your choice

<u>Snack</u>
Protein Bar (KIND BAR)

<u>Dinner</u>
3-4 oz. Steak
½ or whole Sweet Potato (½ tsp Agave Sweetener) Beans

Drink at least 10 glasses of Water a day

Philippians 4:13 I can do all things through him who strengthens me.

<u>Week 1-6 - (Day 3)</u>

<u>Breakfast</u>
1-Scrambled/Fried Egg White (mix in chopped Red Onions/Bell Peppers)
2-pcs Turkey Bacon
1-pc Raisin Bread (Ezekiel Bread/Gluten Free)
½ tsp Almond Butter (Spread on Raisin Bread)

<u>Snack</u> Yogurt
Sm. 5 oz. can Tuna in Water Boiled Egg

<u>Lunch</u>
Sliced Turkey/Grilled Chicken Sliced
Veggie of your choice

<u>Snack</u>
2-pc Turkey Bacon w/mustard 6-8 slices cucumbers

<u>Dinner</u>
3-4 oz. Thin Steak or Chicken Asparagus Spears
Veggie of Your choice or Salad

Drink at least 10 glasses of Water a day

John 15:5 "I am the vine, you are the branches; he who abides in Me and I in him, he bears much fruit, for apart from Me you can do nothing."

Week 1-6 - (Day 4)

Breakfast
1 Scrambled/Fried Egg White (mix in chopped Red Onions & Spinach)
2 pcs Turkey Bacon
1 pc Raisin Bread (Ezekiel Bread/Gluten Free)
½ tsp Almond Butter (Spread on Raisin Bread)

Snack Greek Yogurt
1-pan grilled Turkey Weiner Handful Almonds/Nuts
1 banana

Lunch
Sliced Turkey/Grilled Chicken Sliced
Beans

Snack
1-pc Turkey Bacon w/mustard 6-8 slices cucumbers

Dinner
3-4 oz. Thin Steak (grass fed) or Chicken (organic)
Asparagus Spears
Veggie of Your choice or Salad

Drink at least 10 glasses of Water a day

1 John 1:2 Beloved, I pray that all may go well with you and that you may be in good health, as it goes well with your soul.

Week 1-6 - (Day 5)

Breakfast
1-Scrambled/Fried Egg White 2 pcs Turkey Bacon
1-pc Raisin Bread (Ezekiel Bread/Gluten Free)
(You can make this like 1/2 sandwich (Bread/bacon/egg)

Snack
2-Boiled Egg Whites Handful Almonds/Nuts

Lunch
Fish (Salmon, Tilapia, Catfish) – BAKED, GRILLED, or PAN SEARED ONLY
Spinach
Veggie of your choice

Snack
Protein Bar (KIND BAR)
Or dry popcorn (no butter-Yes moderate Sea Salt)

Dinner
3-4 oz. Baked/Grilled Chicken (Organic)
½ or whole Sweet Potato Veggie of Your Choice

Drink at least 10 glasses of Water a day

Matthew 6:25 "Therefore I tell you, do not be anxious about your life, what you will eat or what you will drink, nor about your body, what you will put on. Is not life more than food, and the body more than clothing?

Week 1-6 - (Day 6)

<u>Breakfast</u>
1-Scrambled Egg White (mix in chopped
Red Onions) 2 pcs Turkey Bacon
1-pc Raisin Bread (Ezekiel Bread/Gluten
Free)
½ tsp Almond Butter (Spread on Raisin
Bread)

<u>Snack</u>
Yogurt
2-pcs Turkey Bacon

<u>Lunch</u>
Turkey/Grilled Chicken/Fish Sliced
Cucumbers or Broccoli Veggie of your
choice

<u>Snack</u>
2 pc Turkey wieners w/mustard 6-8 slices
cucumbers

<u>Dinner</u>
3-4 oz. Thin Steak (grass fed) or Chicken
(Organic) Asparagus Spears
Veggie of Your choice or Salad

Drink at least 10 glasses of Water a day

Proverbs 3:5 *Trust in the Lord with all
your heart, and do not lean on your own
understanding.*

Week 1-6 - (Day 2)

Breakfast
2-Boiled Egg Whites
1-pc Raisin Bread (Ezekiel Bread/Gluten Free)
½ tsp Almond Butter (Spread on Raisin Bread)
1 Organic Banana

Snack
1-Pcs small Turkey Patty w/mustard
Handful Almonds/Nuts

Lunch
Fish (Salmon, Tilapia, Catfish) – BAKED, GRILLED, or PAN SEARED ONLY
Spinach
Veggie of your choice

Snack
Protein Bar (KIND BAR)

Dinner
3-4 oz. Steak
½ or whole Sweet Potato (½ tsp Agave Sweetener) Beans

Drink at least 10 glasses of Water a day

Philippians 4:13 I can do all things through him who strengthens me

<u>**Week 1-6 - (Day 3)**</u>

<u>Breakfast</u>
1-Scrambled/Fried Egg White (mix in chopped Red Onions/Bell Peppers)
2-pcs Turkey Bacon
1-pc Raisin Bread (Ezekiel Bread/Gluten Free)
½ tsp Almond Butter (Spread on Raisin Bread)

<u>Snack</u> Yogurt
Sm. 5 oz. can Tuna in Water Boiled Egg

<u>Lunch</u>
Sliced Turkey/Grilled Chicken Sliced
Veggie of your choice

<u>Snack</u>
2-pc Turkey Bacon w/mustard 6-8 slices cucumbers

<u>Dinner</u>
3-4 oz. Thin Steak or Chicken Asparagus Spears
Veggie of Your choice or Salad

Drink at least 10 glasses of Water a day

John 15:5 "I am the vine, you are the branches; he who abides in Me and I in him, he bears much fruit, for apart from Me you can do nothing."

Week 1-6 - (Day 4)

Breakfast
1 Scrambled/Fried Egg White (mix in chopped Red Onions & Spinach)
2 pcs Turkey Bacon
1 pc Raisin Bread (Ezekiel Bread/Gluten Free)
½ tsp Almond Butter (Spread on Raisin Bread)

Snack Greek Yogurt
1-pan grilled Turkey Weiner Handful Almonds/Nuts
1 banana

Lunch
Sliced Turkey/Grilled Chicken Sliced Beans

Snack
1-pc Turkey Bacon w/mustard 6-8 slices cucumbers

Dinner
3-4 oz. Thin Steak (grass fed) or Chicken (organic) Asparagus Spears Veggie of Your choice or Salad

Drink at least 10 glasses of Water a day

1 John 1:2 Beloved, I pray that all may go well with you and that you may be in good health, as it goes well with your soul.

Week 1-6 - (Day 5)

Breakfast
1-Scrambled/Fried Egg White 2 pcs Turkey
Bacon
1-pc Raisin Bread (Ezekiel Bread/Gluten
Free)
(You can make this like 1/2 sandwich
(Bread/bacon/egg)

Snack
2-Boiled Egg Whites Handful Almonds/Nuts

Lunch
Fish (Salmon, Tilapia, Catfish) – BAKED,
GRILLED, or PAN SEARED ONLY
Spinach
Veggie of your choice

Snack
Protein Bar (KIND BAR)
Or dry popcorn (no butter-Yes moderate
Sea Salt)

Dinner
3-4 oz. Baked/Grilled Chicken (Organic)
½ or whole Sweet Potato Veggie of Your
Choice

Drink at least 10 glasses of Water a day

*Matthew 6:25 "Therefore I tell you, do not
be anxious about your life, what you will eat
or what you will drink, nor about your body,
what you will put on. Is not life more than
food, and the body more than clothing?*

Week 1-6 - (Day 6)

Breakfast
1-Scrambled Egg White (mix in chopped Red Onions) 2 pcs Turkey Bacon
1-pc Raisin Bread (Ezekiel Bread/Gluten Free)
½ tsp Almond Butter (Spread on Raisin Bread)

Snack Yogurt
2-pcs Turkey Bacon

Lunch
Turkey/Grilled Chicken/Fish Sliced Cucumbers or Broccoli Veggie of your choice

Snack
2 pc Turkey wieners w/mustard 6-8 slices cucumbers

Dinner
3-4 oz. Thin Steak (grass fed) or Chicken (Organic) Asparagus Spears
Veggie of Your choice or Salad

Drink at least 10 glasses of Water a day

Proverbs 3:5 Trust in the Lord with all your heart, and do not lean on your own understanding

BODY PROGRESS TRACKER

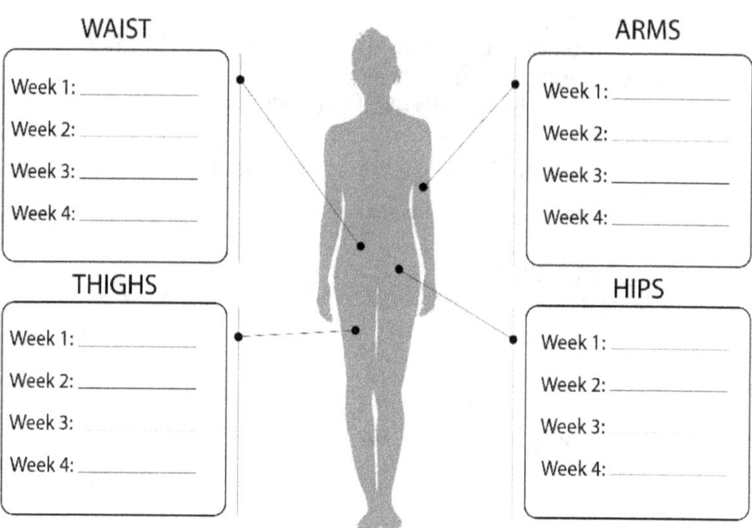

WAIT

Week 1: _______________

Week 2: _______________

Week 3: _______________

Week 4: _______________

ARMS

Week 1: _______________

Week 2: _______________

Week 3: _______________

Week 4: _______________

THIGHS

Week 1: _______________

Week 2: _______________

Week 3: _______________

Week 4: _______________

HIPS

Week 1: _______________

Week 2: _______________

Week 3: _______________

Week 4: _______________

Goal Tracker	Week 1:	Week 2:	Week 3:	Week 4:
DATE				
ARMS				
WAIST				
HIPS				
THIGHS				
WEIGHT				

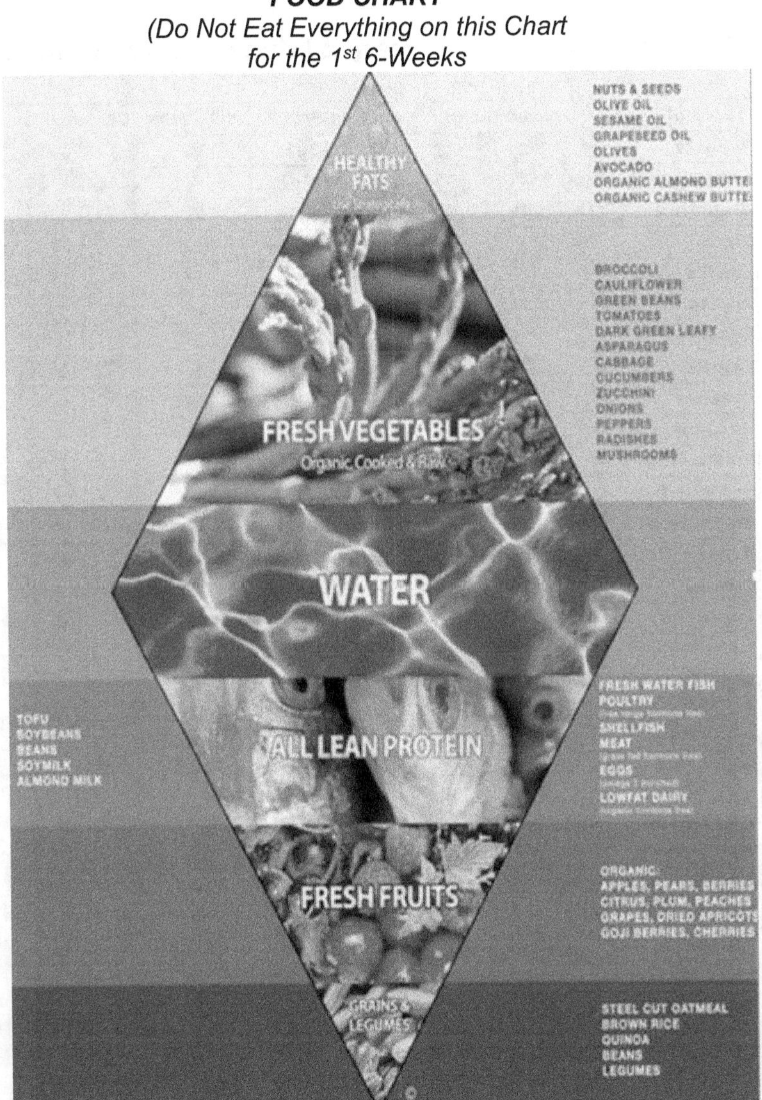

Glycemic Example Chart

Glycemic Index and Glycemic Load of Popular Foods

Green = Low ~ Orange = Medium ~ Red = High

Types of Food	Glycemic Index	Serving Size	Net Carbs	Glycemic Load
Peanuts	14	4 oz (113g)	15	2
Bean sprouts	25	1 cup (104g)	4	1
Grapefruit	25	1/2 large (166g)	11	3
Pizza	30	2 slices (260g)	42	13
Lowfat yogurt	33	1 cup (245g)	47	16
Apples	38	1 medium (138g)	16	6
Spaghetti	42	1 cup (140g)	38	16
Carrots	47	1 large (72g)	5	2
Oranges	48	1 medium (131g)	12	6
Bananas	52	1 large (136g)	27	14
Potato chips	54	4 oz (114g)	55	30
Snickers Bar	55	1 bar (113g)	64	35
Brown rice	55	1 cup (195g)	42	23
Honey	55	1 tbsp (21g)	17	9
Oatmeal	58	1 cup (234g)	21	12
Ice cream	61	1 cup (72g)	16	10
Macaroni and cheese	64	1 serving (166g)	47	30
Raisins	64	1 small box (43g)	32	20
White rice	64	1 cup (186g)	52	33
Sugar (sucrose)	68	1 tbsp (12g)	12	8
White bread	70	1 slice (30g)	14	10
Watermelon	72	1 cup (154g)	11	8
Popcorn	72	2 cups (16g)	10	7
Baked potato	85	1 medium (173g)	33	28
Glucose	100	(50g)	50	50

Nutritional values in this table is courtesy of:
http://nutritiondata.self.com/topics/glycemic-index#ixzz2Jwaw2XZx

GROCERY LIST

Staples:
Pink Himalayan Sea Salt
Olive Oil
Pepper
Mustard
Lemons

Breakfast:
Eggs (Natural/Hormone Free Preferred)
Turkey Bacon
Ezekiel Raisin Bread
Gluten Free Bread
Agave Sweetener
Almond Butter

Fruit:
Tomato
Banana
Lemons
Avocado

Veggies:
Cabbage
Lettuce
Asparagus
Sweet Potatoes
Bell Peppers
Red Onions
Any Veggies you FANCY

Lunch/Dinner:

Chicken (Natural No Hormones)
3-4 oz

Snacks:
Low Calorie String Cheese Almonds/Nuts
Turkey Weiner Protein bars
Yogurt Fage' My preference

Protein
Tuna
Steak (Grass Fed beef) 3-4 oz
Crab Shrimp
Turnkey 3-4 oz. Ground Turkey

Extra's: Sprouted Grain
Gluten

*Places that I purchase items (If you do not have
these places in your hometown then you can
purchase them at your local Wholefoods Market
or similar health food store)

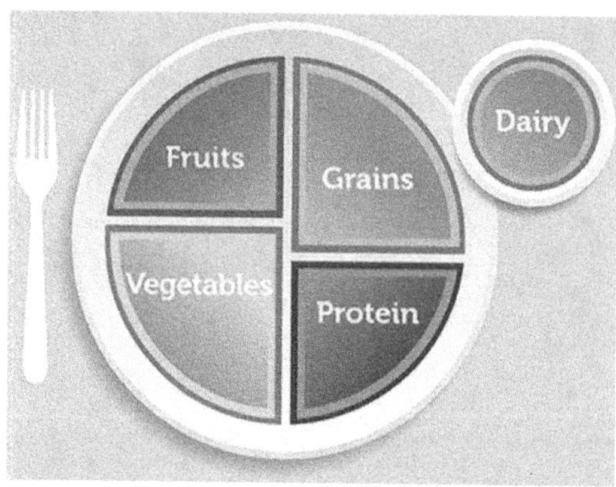

SNACK LIST

Our snack list is very simple. Please do not try to alter it or steer too far from what we have listed, or you may not get the results that we are wanting you to receive from this weight management program.

- Avocado Toast
- Fresh Dry Popcorn (popped from kernels)
- Gluten Free Raisin Bread
- Protein Bar (Kind Bars – My Choice)
- Yogurt (Fage' – My Choice)
- Raw or Roasted Almonds – NO SALT – NO FLAVORING
- Turkey Welner
- Turkey Bacon
- Turkey Patty w/Mustard
- Boiled Egg
- Dry Tuna on a Bed of Lettuce
- LOW FAT 2 % String Cheese

Try to stay away from fruit for the first 6 weeks if possible. If medical conditions warrant you having fruit; then please do as the doctor has requested.

The reason we are saying you should try to stay away from MOST fruit for the first 6 weeks is because the fruit will turn into sugar in your stomach and sugar will turn into fat.

If you <u>MUST</u> eat any fruit, then you can have anything that ends in BERRY.

Example: Strawberry Raspberry Blueberry Blackberry Boysenberry Huckleberry

RECIPES

Avocado Toast

Ingredients:
1 Slice Gluten Free Bread
½ Avocado
Dash Olive Oil
1 Lime wedge
Pink Himalayan Sea Salt
½ tsp cilantro seasoning
Pepper
3-4 small diced fresh Roma Tomatoes
Optional: Red Pepper Flakes and

Instructions:

Slice, then mash the Avocado in a small bowl.
Season mashed avocados with salt, pepper, and cilantro
seasoning. Squeeze Lime wedge into mixture.
Brown bread in toaster. Remove toast from the toaster.
Drizzle toast with Olive Oil.
Spread avocado mixture over toast.
Sprinkle Red Pepper Flakes. Top with Roma Tomatoes. Enjoy.

YouTube: https://youtu.be/sAUFKhaNLe4

Ingredients:
1 cup Popcorn Kernels
1 TBSP Olive Oil

Optional: Sea Salt

Instructions:
Pour about 1 TBSP Olive Oil in a Cooking Pan.

Allow oil heat up.
Put 1 Kernel in the pan and cover until it pops into a popcorn.
Pour 1 layer of kernels in the pan and cover.
Move pan around ever so slightly until almost all kernels have popped or comes to a slow stop.
Season with Sea Salt. Pour into a bowl and
Enjoy.

Ingredients:
Asparagus
Cabbage
Bell Pepper
Purple Onions
Broccoli
½ TBSP Olive Oil
Seasoning

Instructions:

Wash and cut all veggies.
Pour ½TBSP Olive Oil in a Pan.
Allow oil heat until hot.
Add Onions, Bell Pepper, Broccoli, and Asparagus.
Sauté veggies.
Add in remaining veggies, season, and sauté until done.
Enjoy

Ingredients:

Steel Cut Oatmeal
½ Banana Sliced
Blueberries
1 tsp agave nectar
½ tsp cinnamon
1 tsp chia seeds

Instructions:

Cook oatmeal as per directions Slice banana's and put on top
Add Berries
Dash agave. Dash Cinnamon.
Add chia seeds

Ingredients

1 cup Fresh/Frozen Fruit
1 Whole Banana
5 - 6 oz water
1c. fresh/frozen pineapple

Instructions:

Put all ingredients in blender and blend until smooth Add any optional ingredients like spinach or kale
YouTube Video: https://youtu.be/8QJn_E7UUVw

Ingredients

Sweet Potato
Kosher Salt
Olive Oil
Air Fryer Oven

Instructions:

Wash Sweet potatoes. Pierce 5 places w/a knife
Rub Olive Oil over potatoes
Sprinkle with Kosher Salt
Put in air fryer or oven for 35-45 minutes. Enjoy/Skin On

YouTube: Moms On The Go
https://www.youtube.com/watch?v=tYC8tyi-m2I&t=114s

Ingredients:
10 Mini sweet tomatoes
1 medium or large avocado
1 lime
Salt/pepper
Olive oil

Instructions:
Dice tomatoes and Avocado into small chunks.
Squeeze moderate amount of lime juice on mix,
Salt & pepper to taste.
Sprinkle with a little olive oil. Mix and serve.

(only after 1st 6 weeks)

Ingredients:

1 can Garbanzo beans
1 can chunk Chicken (in tuna section) 1 can red kidney beans
1 can black beans
1 can Rotel ™ tomatoes
Seasoning

Instructions:

Open all bean cans and rinse in strainer with tap water Pour
beans, chicken, and Rotel ™ tomatoes into crock pot
2 cans Chicken Broth or 1 carton chicken or veggie broth
Add Seasoning
Heat for approximately 1-2 hours or until hot. Serve
Note: Use any canned beans you wish

Prep Time: 10 min
Cook Time:1-2 hours
Servings: 6-8
YouTube: https://youtu.be/qxiFEoaUZfs

Ingredients
1 bunch kale greens
1/3 cup dried cranberries 1/2 cup slivered almonds
3 TBSP mozzarella cheese

Lemon Vinaigrette Dressing
1 TBSP Dijon Mustard
1 TBSP Fresh Squeezed Lemon
½ tsp salt
$1/8$ tsp pepper
½ tsp Minced Garlic
¼ c. extra virgin olive oil

Instructions:

Wash Kale. Tear off stems.
Slice into small pieces and Massage kale until leaves are soft
Add all ingredients and mix well
Dressing: Mix ingredients in a bowl and Whisk until blended.
Note: You may need judgment, so use to your liking

YouTube: https://youtu.be/8QJn_E7UUVw

Ingredients
1/2 cup extra-virgin olive oil
2 tablespoons fresh lemon juice
1 clove garlic, minced
1 tsp dried basil
½ tsp dried oregano
¼ tsp salt

Instructions:
Combine all ingredients in a blender. Refrigerate until chilled.
Yield: 8 servings (serving size: 1 tablespoon)
Note: This is the BEST dressing ever

Credit: Ultimate Daniel Fast

Ingredients
1 TBSP Turmeric powder
½ tsp cinnamon
1 cup of water or almond milk
1/8 tsp ginger or fresh ginger
1/8 tsp *honey (optional)

Instructions:
Mix and consume
Can be warmed in stock pan or microwave.
Drink at least 3 times per week

Prep Time: 5 min
Servings: 1
(Relieves inflammation, Boost immunity, Arthritis, IBS,
Alzheimer's, & treats and prevents some cancers)

YouTube: https://youtu.be/3xPoiCHhBxQ

Ingredients
Tomatillos
Cilantro
Salt
Dried Arbol Red Peppers
Fresh whole jalapeno pepper
1 Lime
Garlic

Instructions:

WASH and CLEAN ALL VEGGIES FIRST

In a medium sized saucepan put water in the pan and place (cleaned washed) Tomatillos in the water to boil. Add dried Red pepper and jalapeno pepper. Boil until the veggies become soft. It may take about 20 minutes on medium or high.

Next, carefully pour out the water. Put all ingredients in a food processor, add a pinch of salt, about 1/3 of the bunch of cilantros. Make sure you cut off the stems of the cilantro. Squeeze 1/2 of the lime into the food processor, add 2-3 pieces of peeled garlic.

YouTube: https://youtu.be/R-pCzBzzecc

Visit our website for more easy recipes http://www.eat4urlife.com

A FEW FOOD GUIDELINES

We have several guidelines that should be followed within your first 6 weeks of using our weight management program.

#1 Begin making smart choices when eating your meals.
Salads

Only 3-4 ingredients in your salad – NO MORE

- ✓ Lettuce
- ✓ Cucumber
- ✓ Egg White
- ✓ Beets
- ✓ Bell pepper
- ✓ Zucchini
- ✓ Broccoli/Cauliflower

No Salad Dressing – Only Squeeze Fresh Lemon Juice No CHEESE on the SALAD

BEANS

EAT ONLY FRESH DRY BEANS. These can be easily prepared a day or two ahead of time in the Slow Cooker. Beans contain protein so they are very good for you and good for your heart as well.

Meats

When choosing the meats to purchase it is very important that you **try** to stay with products that are as natural as possible.

- ✓ RED Meats should be grass fed beef
- ✓ Chicken (organic/vegetarian diet – Not Fried)
- ✓ Fish (Fresh NOT frozen; baked/steamed NOT Fried)

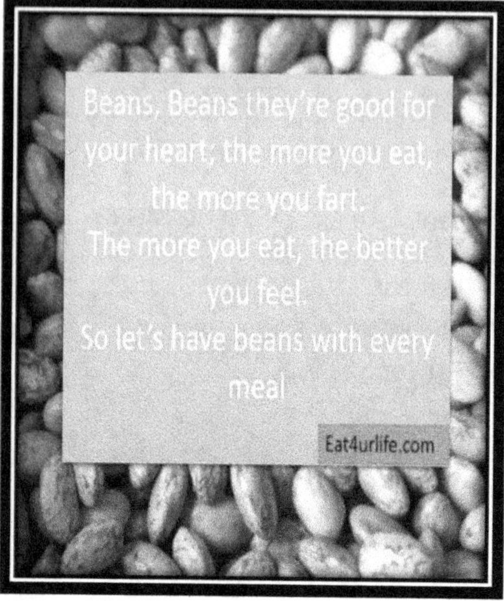
Beans, Beans they're good for
your heart; the more you eat,
the more you fart.
The more you eat, the better
you feel.
So let's have beans with every
meal
Eat4urlife.com

The Importance of Drinking Water

Drinking a healthy amount of water is vital to your health. You can gain tremendous health benefits just by drinking a healthy amount of water. In most cases you can even cure some of your health issues.

The role of water in human body is anywhere from **55% to 78%** water depending on body size. The body consists of 2/3 water; therefore, it is the main component of human body.

Tissues and organs are mainly made up of water?

- ✓ Muscle consists of 75% water
- ✓ Brain consists of 90% of water
- ✓ Bone consists of 22% of water
- ✓ Blood consists of 83% water

Functions of water in human body are extremely vital. Water allows the following functions to take place in your body:

- ✓ Transports nutrients and oxygen into cells
- ✓ Moisturizes the air in lungs
- ✓ Helps with metabolism
- ✓ Protects our vital organ
- ✓ Helps our organs to absorb nutrients better
- ✓ Regulates body temperature
- ✓ Detoxifies
- ✓ Protects and moisturizes our joints

So, you can see that every cell in your body needs water from head to toe. It is very important to drink enough fluid (water). For example, brain consists of 90% water, if you do not supply enough water to your body, your brain cannot function well, and you may develop a headache or migraine. Hence, next time, **if you feel fatigue and headache, it may be the sign of dehydration - - pick up a glass of water and drink up.**

MAKING IT LAST

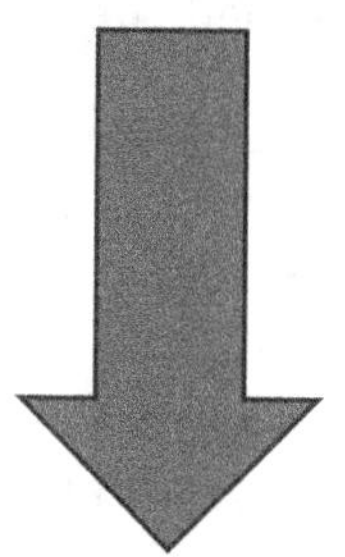

Weight Management App

There are numerous Weight Management Apps on the market that you can download onto your smartphones. The main App

that we currently use to track our progress is My Fitness Pal.

This App is extremely useful. First, start off by downloading it for FREE from your IOS or Android App store. Then you can register your app with all your information. The Application will ask you for your weight and your daily calorie goal. Please make sure you input the most accurate information because the app will begin calculating information based on what you input in your profile.

Finally, input your Breakfast, Lunch, Dinner, and Snacks. It is very simple. In order that you make sure you get the most benefit from your downloaded app you MUST, and I repeat YOU MUST use this app religiously.

Include everything you input in your mouth. My Fitness Pal also allows you to scan barcodes of items that may not be listed in the current database. I absolutely love scanning items into the Application. I feel that I will get more accurate data if I scan the items myself.

Here are some TOP Application features of MyFitnessPal :

- ✓ Calorie tracker
- ✓ Food tracker
- ✓ Weight tracker
- ✓ Facebook Friend Finder
- ✓ Exercise Tracker

✓ Water tracker

MyFitnessPal

As you can see from the screenshots, we previously started out using Herbalife products; but honestly, I felt so hungry throughout the day so I eventually made the choice to do away with the Herbalife Meal replacement shakes.

However, I do feel it's important to find a protein shake that you like so you can get the most benefit from your weight management goals.

Here are some screenshots of our daily food log. We will include more of them in our complete e-book entitled "Eat4urLife Weight Management Plan - - **The Complete Plan for LIFE.**"

App Options Explanation:

Goal - This is the number of Calories that I wanted to take in "1200"

Food – This is the amount of Food Calories that I consumed

Exercise – This is the exercise that I put in the for the day **Net** - Food minus the exercise

Remaining – the calories that I have left over or under for the day

Disclaimer: we do not work for MyfitnessPal – We only discuss this app because we found it to be very useful tracking our food and weight loss goals. We are not being paid for adding them to our eBook.

My Fitness Pal Screenshots

Nonfat Greek Strained Yogurt
Fage Total 0% With Apple Cinnamon Raisins, 150.0 g, 1...   120

Sargento Light String Cheese Sticks (2% Milk)
Yvonne's Casa, 1.0 Stick (21g), 50 cal   50

Lean Turkey Burger Patties 95/5
Jennie O, 1.0 Burger (149g), 160 cal   160

1/4 Cup Almonds
Organic, 1/9 cup whole raw almonds, 26 cal   26

Chocolate Chip
Clif Bar, 0.5 bar (68g), 115 cal   115

Protein Shake
Herbalife Protein Drink Mix, 2.0 scoops, 110 cal   110

CARDIO EXERCISE

Stretching, hatha yoga
60 minutes   208

Elliptical Trainer
20 minutes   250

Stationary bike, light effort (bicycling, cycling, b...   86

DINNER   254 CAL

Organic Raw Almonds
Whole Foods, 1/9 cup (28.4g), 20 cal   20

Iceburg Lettuce Head
Produce Oasis, 72.0 g, 10 cal   10

Fat Free Crab Flavored Seafood
Ralph's, ½ cup (85 grams), 80 cal   80

Baked Sweet Potato (Small)
Sweet Potato Baked Sweet Potato, 1.0 oz, 25 cal   25

Classic Balsamic Vinaigrette With Extra Virgin Ol...
Kraft Salad Dressing, 2.0 tbsp, 90 cal   90

Grilled Red Onions
1/9 cup, 8 cal   8

Grilled Vegetables, Asparagas, Onions, Bell Pepp...
Home Made, 0.5 cup, 0 cal   0

Ready Cooked Rotisserie Chicken
Whole Foods, 0.5 oz, 21 cal   21

Using a Timer

It is important to use a timer when you are managing your new schedule.

It is very important that you eat enough meals throughout the day so that you are <u>not</u> hungry.

You should eat at least 5-6 times a day. The meals that you eat should not be big meals. All meals should be small, but you must plan to eat, or you will have a difficult time losing the weight in the time that we are allotting you to lose.

Most cell phones have timers on them, so you do not have to go out and buy a timer.

Here is what you need to do in a nutshell:

1. After each meal you should set your timer for 2 hours

2. After the timer goes off, you need to eat your snack

It's that simple. Do not skip meals. Your body craves nutrition and to speed up your metabolism you **MUST**

EAT ! Even if you are not hungry

Exercise

You should incorporate exercise into your daily routine. Exercise is important for *many different factors.* Regular exercise is necessary for physical fitness and good health. It reduces the risk of heart disease, cancer, high blood pressure, diabetes, and other diseases. It can improve your appearance and delay the aging process.

There are a million more reasons I can provide about the necessity of exercising.

Ever hear of the phrase "Move it or Lose It?" Well, it is true. If you do not get moving, you may lose movement that you don't need to lose.

Exercise IS Important?

Muscles will become flabby and weak. Your heart and lungs will not function efficiently. And your joints will be stiff and easily injured. Inactivity is as much of a health risk as smoking! Our bodies are meant to move - - so this is one craving that you SHOULD give into.

START SLOW

If you are a beginner, start off slower than you think you should. Three days per week is realistic, safe, and effective. If you are experienced, do cardiovascular (aerobic) exercises such as walking, jogging, and bicycling for no more than 200 minutes per week with no more than 60 minutes per session.

Lemon water has many health benefits. Very little scientific research has been done specifically on lemon water, so we can't state a lot of medical facts, but we do know there are great benefits.

Benefits of Lemon Water:

1. Good Source of Vitamin C
2. Promotes Hydration
3. Supports Weight Loss
4. Improves Skin Quality
5. Aids in Digestion
6. Wards off certain cancers
7. Helps prevent kidney stones
8. Assists you in drinking more water

Side effects of lemon water

1. Lemon water safe to drink, but there are a few potential side effects:

As we already know, Lemons contain citric acid, which may erode tooth enamel. This risk can be limited by, drinking lemon water through a straw, and rinse your mouth with plain water afterwards.

2. Some people may experience heartburn after drinking lemon water. Get to know your body. This side effect may disappear after the first few initial drinks.

Lemon water has various potential health benefits. Also, adding lemon to your water may help you drink more throughout the day. Lemon water is hydration, so drink up.

Ingredients:
1 Lemon Wedge
1/8 tsp natural honey (optional)

Instructions:

Warm water in kettle or in a mug in microwave
Squeeze lemon wedge into water
Add honey (optional) and stir.
Sip and ENJOY !

REMINDER: Don't forget to brush your teeth or rinse your mouth with cool water after drinking lemon water. Also, you can drink your lemon water through a straw, but be careful not to burn your tongue.

Our Contact Information

You are not in this process alone. We would love to help motivate you and keep you on the right track. Please feel free to contact us with any questions that you may have. We are here to help.

Email: Eat4urlifeplan@gmail.com
Website: http://www.eat4urlife.com
Twitter: http://www.twitter.com/Eat4urlife
FB:https://www.facebook.com/eat4urlife
IG:http://instagram.com/eat4urlifeplan#
YouTube:http://www.youtube.com/user/eat4urlifeplan

Thank you for your purchase

30-Day Money-Back Guarantee

If you're not satisfied with your results within **30 days**, simply call Customer Service for a Return Authorization number to return the program for the full purchase price.

LEGAL DISCLAIMER

All information and tools presented within this eBook/website are intended for educational purposes. Any health, diet or exercise advice is <u>not</u> intended as medical diagnosis or treatment. If you think you have any type of medical condition you must seek professional advice even if you believe it may be due to diet, food or

exercise. Eat4urlife.com is not a medical institute and therefore none of its staff will give any diagnosis or medical advice. By purchasing our eBook & using our site you agree to our terms.

Eat4urlife.com was established to provide good, practical information to help <u>healthy adults</u> in their weight loss efforts.

This site is not intended for people under 18

years, pregnant or breast-feeding women, underweight individuals or people with eating disorders or any health condition that requires a special diet. We do not guarantee that the information will be completely accurate. Therefore, the author, publisher or and owners cannot be held responsible for any errors, omissions or inaccuracies published. It is advised that all visitors check information provided on this site with a professional source.

The owners, distributors and any participants disclaim all liability or loss in conjunction with any content provided here. We disclaim any liability for products or services recommended on the eat4urlife.com site including defective products or direct, indirect, special, incidental or consequential damages, arising out of the use or the inability to use the materials/information published or products sold on this site.

YOU SHOULD ALWAYS CONSULT A QUALIFIED PRACTITIONER BEFORE USING ANY DIETARY, EXERCISE OR HEALTH ADVICE FROM THIS eBook or SITE!

We urge all our web site visitors to seek medical / professional advice before beginning any weight loss program, exercise, training regime or any diet. When embarking on any training program we also urge people to start slowly and gradually.

Always select exercises that are safe. If you experience discomfort, distress or any other symptom while exercising please do not continue. Listen to your body.

WE RESPECT THE SAFETY AND WELLBEING OF VISITORS THEREFORE WE DO NOT PROVIDE ANY DIAGNOSIS OR MEDICAL ADVICE.

All information contained within this website is the property of Eat4urlife.com and is not to be used without written authorization from the owner. All product names and trademarks mentioned in any part of the website belong to their respective owners. The information on this page may NOT be accurate, therefore you should NOT take any of the content as a source of reference for any reason whatsoever!

You are responsible for comparing the information with an accurate source before using any, or part of this content

BODY PROGRESS TRACKER

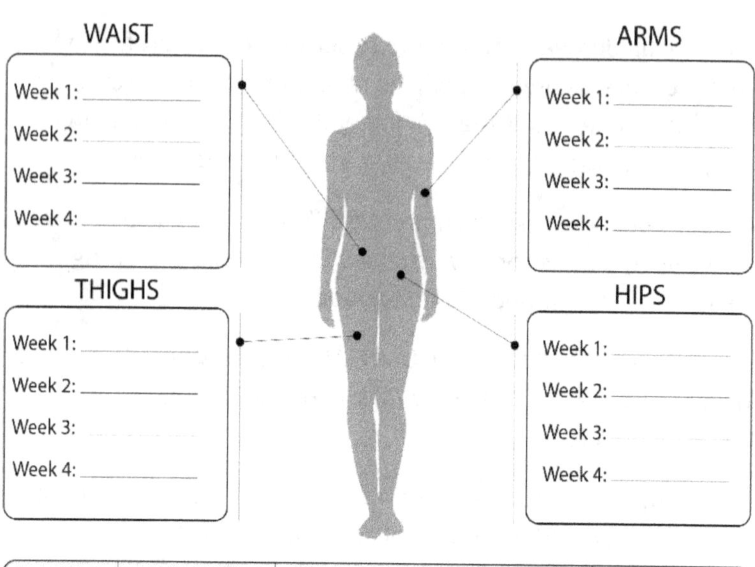

Goal Tracker	Week 1:	Week 2:	Week 3:	Week 4:
DATE				
ARMS				
WAIST				
HIPS				
THIGHS				
WEIGHT